MAKE-IT MODELS

MAKE A
BIOSPHERE AND MINI GARDEN

Anna Claybourne

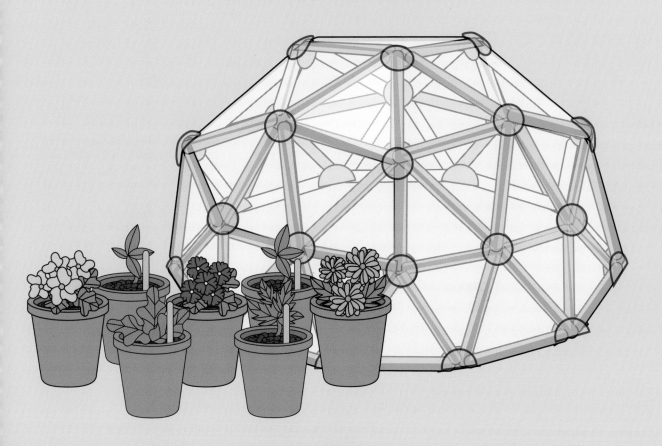

CRABTREE
PUBLISHING COMPANY
WWW.CRABTREEBOOKS.COM

CRABTREE
PUBLISHING COMPANY
WWW.CRABTREEBOOKS.COM

Published in Canada
Crabtree Publishing
616 Welland Avenue
St. Catharines, ON
L2M 5V6

Published in the United States
Crabtree Publishing
PMB 59051
350 Fifth Ave, 59th Floor
New York, NY 10118

Published in 2020 by Crabtree Publishing Company

First published in Great Britain in 2019 by Wayland
Copyright © Hodder and Stoughton, 2019

Author: Anna Claybourne

Editorial director: Kathy Middleton

Editors: Elise Short, Elizabeth DiEmanuele

Proofreader: Wendy Scavuzzo

Design and illustration: Collaborate

Production coordinator and prepress: Ken Wright

Print coordinator: Katherine Berti

Printed in the U.S.A./122019/CG20191101

The website addresses (URLs) included in this book were valid at the time of going to press. However, it is possible that contents or addresses may have changed since the publication of this book. No responsibility for any such changes can be accepted by either the author or the Publisher.

Note: In preparation of this book, all due care has been exercised with regard to the instructions, activities, and techniques depicted. The publishers regret that they can accept no liability for any loss or injury sustained. Always get adult supervision and follow manufacturers' advice when using electric and battery-powered appliances.

Library and Archives Canada Cataloguing in Publication

Title: Make a biosphere and mini-garden / Anna Claybourne.
Other titles: Biosphere and mini garden
Names: Claybourne, Anna, author.
Description: Series statement: Make-it models |
  Previously published under title: Biosphere and mini garden.
  London: Wayland, 2019. | Includes index.
Identifiers: Canadiana (print) 20190200316 |
  Canadiana (ebook) 20190200324 |
  ISBN 9780778773528 (hardcover) |
  ISBN 9780778773580 (softcover) |
  ISBN 9781427124913 (HTML)
Subjects: LCSH: Greenhouses—Models—Juvenile literature. |
  LCSH: Gardens—Models—Juvenile literature. |
  LCSH: Models and modelmaking—Juvenile literature.
Classification: LCC SB416 .C53 2020 |
  DDC j690/.89240228—dc23

Library of Congress Cataloging-in-Publication Data

Names: Claybourne, Anna, author.
Title: Make a biosphere and mini-garden / Anna Claybourne.
Description: New York : Crabtree Publishing Company, 2020. |
  Series: Make-it models | Includes index.
Identifiers: LCCN 2019043975 (print) |
  LCCN 2019043976 (ebook) |
  ISBN 9780778773528 (hardcover) |
  ISBN 9780778773580 (paperback) |
  ISBN 9781427124913 (ebook)
Subjects: LCSH: Biosphere—Juvenile literature. |
  Gardens—Juvenile literature. | Handicraft—Juvenile literature.
  | Biology projects—Juvenile literature.
Classification: LCC QH343.4 .C53 2020 (print) |
  LCC QH343.4 (ebook) | DDC 333.95--dc23
LC record available at https://lccn.loc.gov/2019043975
LC ebook record available at https://lccn.loc.gov/2019043976

CONTENTS

GROW A GARDEN

Gardens come in all shapes and sizes, from tiny window boxes to parks and **botanical gardens**. They add color to the world with flowers, and help wildlife by providing food and shelter for insects and birds. People use their gardens to grow fruit and vegetables, or just as a place to relax and play.

If you love growing things and being creative, this book is for you. It shows you how to make your own mini model garden or **biosphere** with real plants. The biosphere is everything that is alive on Earth. But a human-made biosphere is a building in which the biosphere is recreated, such as a rain forest or woodland.

It could also be a great garden for toys. They can sit out on the mini benches and seats, have a sleepover in the summer house, or go for a swim in the fountain.

NO GARDEN? NO PROBLEM!

Not everyone is lucky enough to have their own real garden. If you do have one, you might be able to use a corner of it for your model mini garden. If not, your garden can also be made indoors, near a sunny window, in a porch, on a veranda, or on a balcony, as long as there's a bit of space you have permission to use.

MAKE-IT MATERIALS

For the projects in this book, you'll need some basic gardening equipment and materials, such as potting soil and seeds. You can find these at a garden center, or at a big grocery store (especially in spring and summer). You don't need lots of expensive stuff. For example, old yogurt containers or ice-cream tubs make good plant pots.

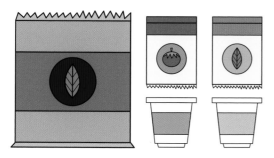

Some projects use household items and craft materials, such as old food containers, glue, modeling clay, and wooden craft sticks. You can find most items at a toy store or craft store. Go to page 31 for a list of useful sources.

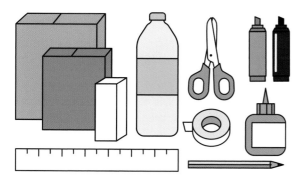

Go to page 31 for a list of useful sources.

Thrift stores are a place to look for household items and materials too.

SAFETY ALERT!

For some of the projects, you will need to use sharp tools, such as a craft knife or a bradawl (a pointed tool for making holes), or an electric appliance, such as a hot **glue gun**.

For anything involving sharp objects, heat, or electricity, always ask an adult to help and supervise. Make sure you keep items like these in a safe place.

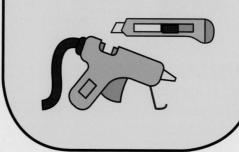

WATCH OUT FOR PETS!

If possible, put your garden somewhere pets can't go, because they could easily knock over or mess up your creations. Unfortunately, when dogs and cats see soil, they sometimes like to poop in it! So keep them away, if you can.

CAN I USE THIS?

Before you start emptying the cupboards, make sure you have permission to use the items for your creations. Now, you're ready to get gardening!

GARDEN BASE

Your mini garden needs a place to sit. If it's outdoors, it could go on a flat area of garden. If it's indoors or on a balcony, it needs some kind of tray or container. Here are three options. Choose the one that works best for you.

WHAT YOU NEED

- A small area of garden lawn or bare soil
- Pebbles or sticks

Option 1: Outdoor space

Best if you have an outdoor area of grassy ground or soil. (Remember this garden will get rained on, so some of your models might not last as long as they would indoors.)

1 If possible, choose a sunny location in a corner or next to a wall or fence because it won't be as windy. Make sure you have permission to use the space.

2 Your garden can be any shape. You can make it big or small. A good size is about 28–32 inches (70–80 cm) square or a 20 by 39 inch (50 by 100 cm) rectangle.

3 Use sticks or pebbles to make a border around the edge of your garden area, so everyone knows where it is.

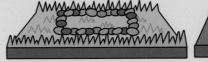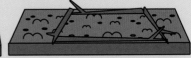

Option 2: Indoor or outdoor garden tray

Best if: you have an indoor area or a sheltered outdoor area, such as a covered balcony with a hard surface.

1 Unless you have one already, you will need to buy the tray from a garden center or order one online, so this option is more expensive. Look for a tray around 28–32 inches (70–80 cm) square or 20 by 39 inches (50 by 100 cm). It should be hard plastic with no holes.

2 Put the tray in a safe, sunny spot. Pour in a bag of sand, such as play sand from a toy shop or gardening sand from a garden center. Evenly spread the sand out.

WHAT YOU NEED

- A large garden **drip tray** or **hydroponics** tray
- A bag of sand

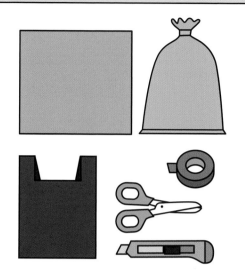

WHAT YOU NEED

- A large cardboard box, or piece of cardboard
- Scissors or craft knife
- A garbage bag or a waterproof garden sack
- Clear tape
- A bag of sand

Option 3: Indoor homemade tray

Best if you need something cheaper than option 2! This will only work somewhere that won't get any rain on it because it will get soggy.

1 **Option A:** With an adult's help, cut the sides off of a large cardboard box to make a large tray, 3 inches (8 cm) deep. Strengthen any loose parts with tape.

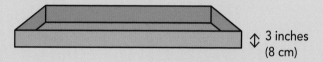

3 inches (8 cm)

Option B: If you have flat cardboard, fold the edges up about 3 inches (8 cm) in to make sides. At the corners, cut the cardboard so that the sides can overlap. Tape them together.

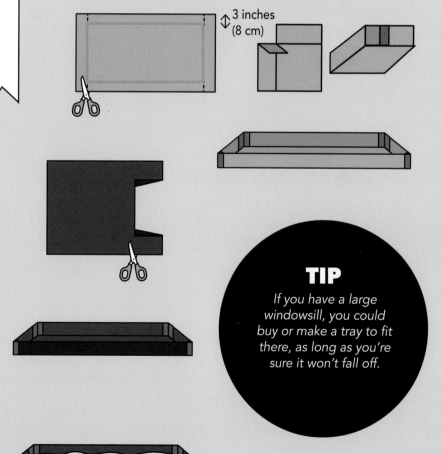

3 inches (8 cm)

2 Lay the garbage bag flat. Carefully cut off the base and the handles if there are any. Cut along one side, then open up the bag into a large sheet.

3 Use the opened bag to make a waterproof lining for your tray, making sure it fits into all the sides and corners. Fold it over the edges, and tape it onto the outside of the tray.

4 Put the tray in a safe, sunny spot. Pour in a bag of sand, such as play sand from a toy store or gardening sand from a garden center. Evenly spread out the sand.

TIP

If you have a large windowsill, you could buy or make a tray to fit there, as long as you're sure it won't fall off.

GRASS ART

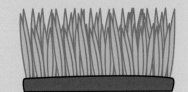

Make grass art! It could be a letter or word, a shape or symbol, a face, a maze, or whatever else you want.

WHAT YOU NEED

- A large, shallow plant container or clean food tray
- A bradawl or a sewing needle
- An eraser or a cork
- Potting soil
- A small packet of grass seed
- Paper and a pencil
- Scissors
- Paper towels
- A large plate
- A fork
- A spray bottle or a small watering can (optional)
- Small pebbles or shells (optional)

Search for a "patch pack" of grass seed. This only contains a small amount of seed and is cheaper.

1 Make sure your plant container or food tray has drainage holes. If it doesn't, ask an adult to make some by pushing a bradawl or sewing needle through the base a few times, into an eraser or cork on the other side.

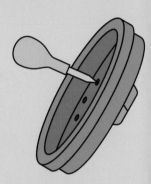

2 Turn the container upside down. Draw around it on a piece of paper to give you the exact size and shape. Draw the design for your grass art inside the shape. It needs to be very simple and clear. Avoid small details, because they won't show up. Here are some ideas:

A star

A smiley face

A letter

Your hand

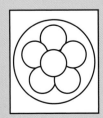

A flower

A simple grass maze

3 Put the container into your garden area or tray, so that it can drain onto to the ground or the sand. Pour soil into it. Break up and flatten down the soil using a fork. Do this until the container is almost full to the top.

4 Cut out your design. On a piece of paper towel, trace around the cutout. Cut it out carefully. Put the paper towel shape (or shapes) on the plate. Sprinkle or spray it with water until it's soaked. With dry hands, sprinkle grass seed all over it.

5 Carefully pick up the wet, seed-covered paper towel (this might be easier with two people). Lay it on the soil in the container. Pick off any grass seeds that have fallen off.

6 Carefully sprinkle more soil over the shape, so that it's covered in a shallow layer about 0.5 inches (1 cm) deep. Water the soil gently, with a small watering can or spray bottle if possible. Keep it damp by watering it lightly every day.

7 After a week, your grass should start to grow in the shape you made. If you want, you can cover the spaces in between with small pebbles or shells. You can also trim the grass with scissors if it gets too long.

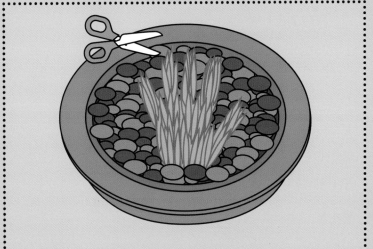

BEAN TREE

Bean plants are easy to grow and fast-growing, they have beautiful flowers, and best of all, they give you beans! Since your model garden is small, your bean plants will tower over it like trees.

WHAT YOU NEED

- A packet of bean seeds (such as broad bean, or French bean)
- A clean, empty glass jar
- Paper towels
- Potting soil
- A medium-sized plant pot, or other container, such as an old ice-cream tub
- A bradawl or a sewing needle
- A spoon
- Three **plant sticks**, or any long, thin, straight sticks
- A rubber band or string
- A plastic bottle or small empty yogurt container
- Scissors
- A small watering can or a spray bottle (optional)

When buying your seeds, search for **dwarf varieties** or "dwarf beans." They are smaller than normal and will fit your garden better.

1 Tear off two to three pieces of paper towel. Fold them up to make a wad of paper that will fit inside your jar. Push the paper towel into the jar so that it is pressed against the sides.

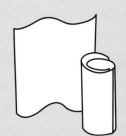

2 Push three bean seeds down in between the paper towel and the glass, spacing them evenly around the jar. Sprinkle or spray the paper towel with water until it's soaked through.

3 Put the jar in a warm place, such as a sunny windowsill. Sprinkle or spray it every day to keep the paper towel damp. In a few days, the bean seeds should start to sprout roots and shoots.

4 If your plant pot or container doesn't have any holes in the bottom, ask an adult to make some by pushing the bradawl or sewing needle through the base a few times.

5 Fill the plant pot with soil, pressing it down to make it firm. Make a hole in the middle with the spoon.

6 Choose the **seedling** that looks strongest and greenest. Gently take it out of the jar. Lower the root into the hole in the soil. When the bean is just below the surface, press the soil together around the shoot.

7 Take your three sticks. Push them into the soil in a triangle around the edge of the pot. At the top, tie the three sticks together with string or a rubber band.

8 Over the sticks, put a small empty yogurt container or a small plastic bottle with the top cut off over the sticks. Don't skip this step. It stops the sticks from accidentally poking someone in the eye!

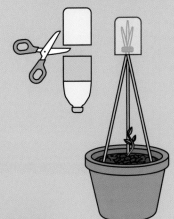

9 Put the bean pot in your garden. Water the compost a little every day. The bean plant should grow quite quickly and climb up the sticks. If you're lucky, it will grow flowers, then bean pods with beans inside.

TAKE IT FURTHER

If you have enough pots and soil, you can plant other beans!

THE SCIENCE PART!

Like other plants, bean seeds need water and warmth to sprout. Once they have leaves, they grow using sunlight, water, and **carbon dioxide** gas from the air. This process is called **photosynthesis**.

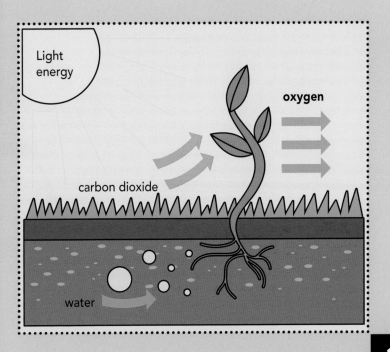

Light energy

oxygen

carbon dioxide

water

WILDFLOWER CORNER

Gardeners often grow exotic flowers that are made for gardens, such as roses, lilies, or clematis. **Wildflowers** are different. These are flowers that grow naturally in places such as parks and country meadows. They grow in gardens, too, if you give them a chance!

WHAT YOU NEED

- A packet of wildflower seeds
- Gravel or small pebbles
- Larger pebbles or sticks
- Potting soil
- A fork
- A spray bottle or small watering can (optional)

You can buy packets of mixed wildflower seeds at garden centers or grocery stores; however, you may be able to collect some wild seeds, too. Go to the pink box on page 13 to find out how.

1 **Option A:** If your garden is outdoors on an area of grass or soil, you don't need the gravel. Pour potting soil on the corner or end of your garden, pressing it down and shaping it into a flower bed.

Option B: If your garden is on a tray, in a corner or end of the tray, trace the outline of your flower bed in the sand. Spread a layer of gravel or small pebbles over the sand in this area. This helps the water drain away. Cover it with a deeper layer of soil.

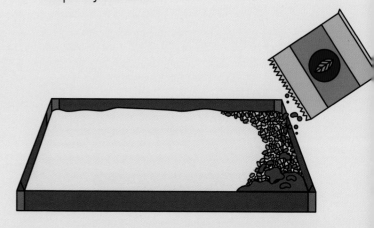

2 Arrange sticks or pebbles along the edge of your flower bed to make a border. This will look nice and also help to hold the soil in place.

3 Gently sprinkle the wildflower seeds evenly over the soil. Then use the fork to rake and turn over the surface, so the seeds are covered with soil.

4 Gently water the soil with a small watering can or spray bottle, or sprinkle it with water using your fingers. Do this every day to keep the soil damp. The plants should start to grow in a few days.

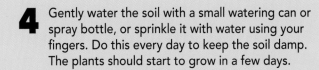

COLLECTING WILD SEEDS

In late summer, wildflowers, such as poppies, clovers, buttercups, and chicory, make their seeds. If you see any of these plants, you can collect their seeds in a paper bag and plant them in your garden. Just take a few, so the plants have some seeds left.

Poppies have little lantern-shaped **seedpods**. Gently shake the seeds from inside the pod into your bag.

Poppy   Seed pod

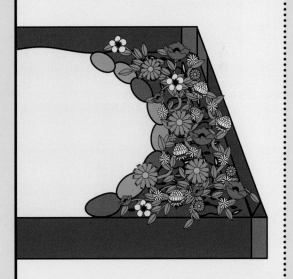

Many flowers develop dry, brownish **seed heads**, like these. Hold the seed head inside your paper bag and shake it until some seeds fall off.

Buttercup   Chicory   Clover

Seed head   Seed head   Seed head

THE SCIENCE PART!

If your garden is outdoors, the wildflowers will provide food and resting places for bees, butterflies, and other wildlife. It's a good idea for all gardens to have a wildflower corner, to help the plants and animals that live near by.

GEODESIC DOME GREENHOUSE

A geodesic dome is a round structure made of many geometric shapes. Domes like this can be used to make tents, but they are great for biospheres or **greenhouses** because they are strong and provide lots of space.

WHAT YOU NEED

- A package of thin craft sticks, 4.4 inches (11.3 cm) in length (you will need about 70 of them)
- A calculator
- A ruler and a pencil
- Scissors and a craft knife
- A button or large coin about 1 inch (2.5 cm) wide
- Cardboard
- Superglue or a hot glue gun
- Clear acetate (a type of plastic sheet you can get from a craft store or old packaging)
- A marker
- A disposable plastic bottle (optional)

1 First, you need to prepare your craft sticks because you will need two different lengths— full-length and shorter. The shorter sticks need to be 3.8 inches (9.6 cm) in length. Use the ruler and pencil to mark this length on 30 sticks.

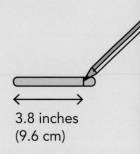

3.8 inches (9.6 cm)

2 Now cut the sticks off at the marked line. You may be able to do this with strong scissors. Otherwise, ask an adult to use a craft knife to cut along the line. Then snap the stick neatly.

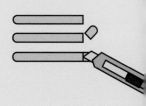

3 Put 30 shorter sticks in a pile and 35 full-length sticks in another pile. In these pictures, we've used different colors to identify the two lengths of sticks.

Short sticks

Long sticks

4 Place the coin or button onto cardboard and draw around it 21 times to make 21 circles. Cut them out. Cut five of them neatly in half to make 10 semicircles.

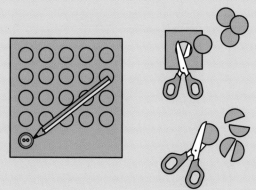

5 Start building your dome. First, take 10 longer sticks (shown in turquoise) and arrange them into a circular base, like this.

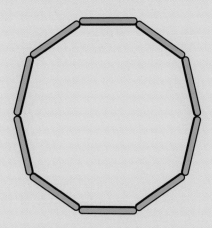

6 Take a cardboard semicircle and glue a stick on each side of the semicircle to link the sticks together. Do this all the way around the circle. The semicircle should be on the inside of the circle of sticks.

7 Use two more long sticks to make a triangle on top of one of the base sticks. Glue them on the semicircles at each side, and make them meet at the top. Join the sticks by gluing them onto a cardboard circle.

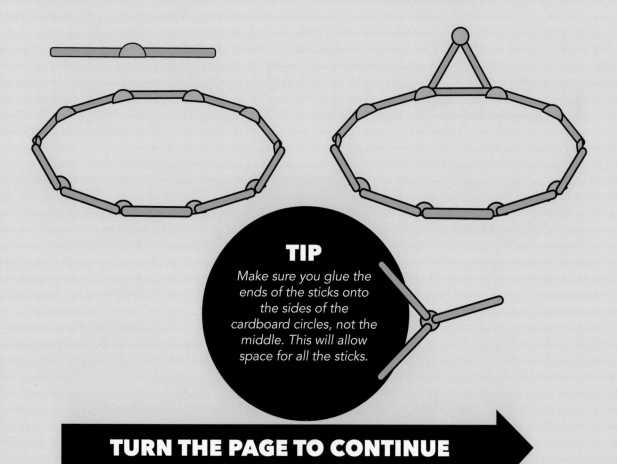

TIP
Make sure you glue the ends of the sticks onto the sides of the cardboard circles, not the middle. This will allow space for all the sticks.

TURN THE PAGE TO CONTINUE

8 Make another triangle the same way on the next base stick, but use two of the shorter sticks instead (shown in orange).

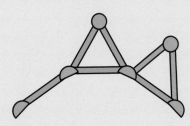

9 Keep working around the circle, alternating the triangles with short and long sticks.

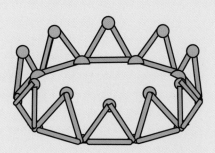

10 Find one of the triangles made with short sticks. Use two more short sticks and glue to connect the top of this triangle to the tops of the triangles on each side.

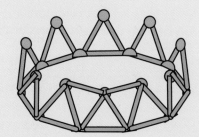

11 Then add a third short stick on the top of the triangle, pointing straight upward. Repeat steps 11 and 12 with all five of the short triangles around the dome.

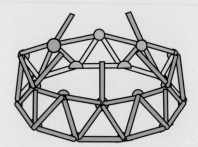

12 Next, use two long sticks, one cardboard circle, and glue to connect the upright stick to the sticks on each side. Do this all the way around, so you have five **pentagon** shapes made from the long sticks.

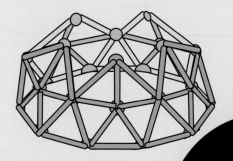

13 Use five long sticks and glue to connect the tops of the pentagons together in a circle. Finally, use five short sticks to make the top of the dome, with one cardboard circle in the middle.

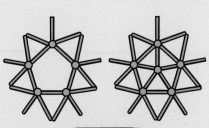

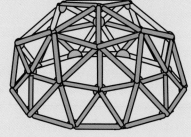

TIP

As you work, you'll find that you have to push the sticks inward to make them join up. You will see the dome shape start to appear.

14 Now you can add the greenhouse "glass." Take a piece of acetate. Hold it against the dome. Use a marker to draw along the sticks to copy the shape of a triangle. Draw the triangle shapes close together on the pieces of acetate so you don't waste any.

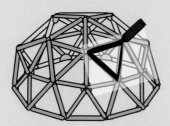

15 Cut out the triangle. Carefully glue its edges onto the sticks to make a window. Repeat steps 14 and 15 for all the other triangles in the dome.

16 This step is optional. Take your coin or button. Draw around it with a marker onto your plastic bottle 21 times. Cut out the 21 circles with scissors and cut five of them in half.

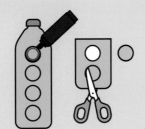

17 Carefully glue the plastic semicircles and circles in the same places as the matching cardboard pieces. You don't have to do this, but it will make the dome look neater and help to keep light rain out.

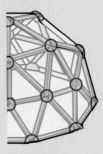

THE SCIENCE PART!

Greenhouses are used to grow plants that like warm temperatures. As sunlight shines into the greenhouse, it heats up the air and soil inside.

Most of the heat reflects back off of the glass. The hot air can't escape, so the temperature inside ends up hotter than outside.

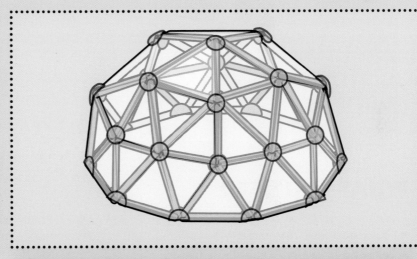

TAKE IT FURTHER

If you like making geodesic domes, you could make several of them in different sizes or try making connected domes.

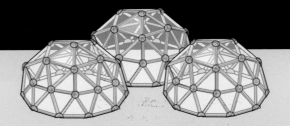

GREENHOUSE GARDEN

Use your geodesic greenhouse to grow some vegetables, which you can then harvest and eat. To get the best results, whether it's indoors or outdoors, put your greenhouse dome in the sunniest possible spot.

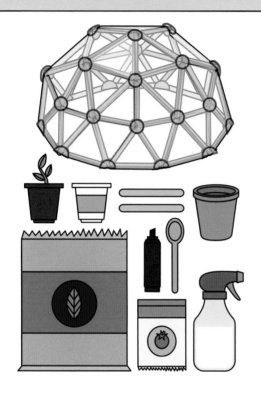

WHAT YOU NEED

- Your geodesic dome greenhouse
- Vegetable seeds or seedlings from a grocery store or garden center (see box on the right for tips)
- Small plant pots or empty yogurt containers
- Potting soil
- A spoon
- Wooden craft sticks or strips of cardboard
- A marker
- A spray bottle or a small watering can (optional)

GREENHOUSE PLANTS

You can either plant your vegetables and flowers from seeds or buy ready-grown seedlings that will grow bigger in your greenhouse. Either way, search for dwarf varieties so they stay nice and small!

Good plants to try are:
- Tomatoes
- Mild chili peppers
- Lettuce
- Herbs, such as coriander, basil, and parsley

1 Pick a place to put your geodesic greenhouse in your mini garden. Make sure it's in a place where it will be in full sun for at least some of the day.

2 Arrange your small pots in the space you've picked, then put the dome over them to check that they fit. Don't pack them too tightly together.

3 Take the dome off again and fill the pots with soil. Press it down firmly with the spoon.

4 If you're using seeds, follow the instructions on the packets. Plant a few seeds in each pot, then water them until the soil is damp.

5 If you're using seedlings, water them while they are still in their containers and leave them for a few minutes. Use the spoon to dig out a space in the soil in each pot.

6 Carefully lift out each seedling and push its roots and soil into the space in the pot. Gently press down the soil around the base of the plant. Water it a bit more.

7 As you do your planting, write the name of each type of plant on a craft stick or strip of cardboard to make a marker. Push it down the side of the plant pot so you will know the name of each plant.

8 Put the dome back over the plants. Take it off each day to water the plants and check how they are doing.

TIP

When you have ripe vegetables or herbs, you can pick them off. Wash them well before eating!

TAKE IT FURTHER

If you don't want to grow vegetables or herbs, you could try some hothouse flowers instead. Flowers that like a nice warm greenhouse include geraniums, nasturtiums, dahlias, and marigolds.

FOUNTAIN

All of the best gardens have a beautiful fountain. The sound of flowing water adds a peaceful atmosphere and some fountains have fish in them, too.

WHAT YOU NEED

- A clear plastic food bowl, such as a salad bowl
- A bradawl (a tool for boring holes) or thick needle
- Cardboard
- A marker and a pencil
- Scissors and a craft knife
- Several bendy straws
- Superglue
- Clear tape
- A large disposable plastic bottle with a lid
- A small plastic bottle with a spout lid
- Flat plastic packaging, such as an ice-cream tub lid
- A jug
- Modeling clay or air-drying clay
- A cooking syringe or squeeze bottle
- Paints, paintbrushes, and white glue (optional)
- Lots of buttons, beads, sequins, or small pebbles (optional)

You can find small bottles with spout lids in most pharmacies, if you don't have any at home.

1 If you want to paint your fountain, do this first. Mix your paint color with an equal amount of white glue. Paint the outside of your plastic bowl and leave it to dry.

2 Make a hole at the bottom of the plastic bowl by pushing the bradawl or sewing needle through it. The hole should be right in the middle. Make the hole larger with a pencil, until it is the same width as a straw.

3 Trace the base of the bowl onto cardboard. Cut the circle out and draw a smaller circle in the middle, about 2 inches (5 cm) across. Cut this circle out, then cut a piece out of the side of the circle to make a channel. Your circle will now look like a C.

4 Using the bendy part, make a right angle with your straw. Working from under the bowl, push the short end through the hole in the bowl from below. Put super glue around the straw where it comes through the hole to seal it. Push the longer end of another straw into the top of the short end, squeezing it slightly to make it fit. Wrap clear tape around the join.

5 Push the longer end of a third straw into the longer end of the first straw under the bowl the same way. Tape them together. Now sit the bowl on the circle of cardboard, so that the straw fits into the channel. Glue the bowl to the cardboard.

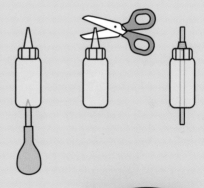

6 With the bradawl or needle, make a hole in the side of the large bottle near the base, the same width as a straw. Push the end of the straw into the bottle. Put glue around the hole, then add tape to seal.

7 Take your small bottle and make a hole in its base, bigger than the width of a straw. Use strong scissors or a craft knife to cut off the tip of the spout so a straw can also fit through.

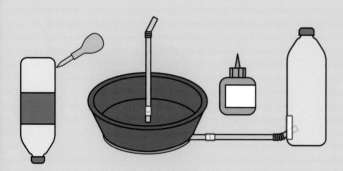

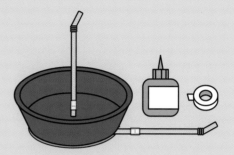

8 Fit the bottle over the straw in the middle of the fountain, so that the straw sticks up through the spout. Trim the straw off just above the spout.

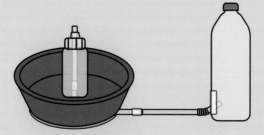

TIP

Avoid using a hot glue gun on plastic bottles and bowls, as they may melt. Use glue instead.

TURN THE PAGE TO CONTINUE ➜

9 Draw a circle onto your plastic packaging, about 4 inches (10 cm) across. Cut it out and make a hole in the middle, slightly larger than the spout on the bottle. Fit the circle over the spout. Use a bit of superglue to hold it in place.

10 When the glue has dried, test your fountain. Ask someone to pinch the straw next to the large bottle, while you use the jug to fill the bottle with water to the top. Screw the lid on tightly, then have the person let go of the straw. To make the fountain flow, unscrew the lid a bit. To stop it, tighten the lid.

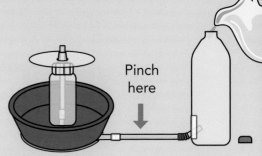

Pinch here

11 To get the water out of the fountain, suck it up using a cooking syringe or squeeze bottle. Squirt it back into the jug to use it again.

12 Take out your modeling clay or air-drying clay and roll it into a long, thick rectangle.

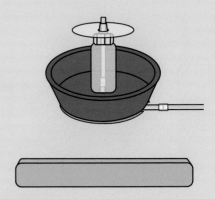

13 Wrap the clay around the bowl to make a wall around the fountain, slightly overlapping the bowl around the top edge. Smooth the clay where it joins together and shape it the way you want.

14 If you want, add a mosaic design to the fountain by pushing beads, buttons, sequins, or small pebbles into the clay. Arrange them randomly or create a pattern or color scheme.

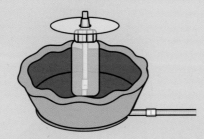

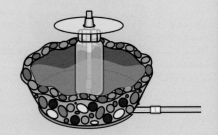

15 If you're using air-drying clay, wait for it to dry before using the fountain. You can now carefully move your fountain into position in your garden, with the water bottle nearby.

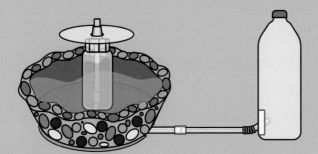

THE SCIENCE PART!

Water can only flow from the bottle into the fountain when air can get in to replace it. When the lid is loosened, air pressure pushes the water down and out of the fountain. When the lid is tightened, the water stops flowing.

TIP

If you want the fountain to spout higher, leave the lid on and squeeze the large bottle.

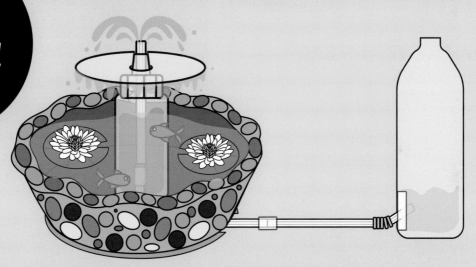

TAKE IT FURTHER

- Make lily pads to float in your fountain by cutting pad shapes out of green craft foam. You could make flowers from white and yellow foam too.
- Use orange modeling clay to make some goldfish!

23

SUMMER HOUSE

A summer house is a little building in a garden where you can sit and read or have a picnic. You can make a summer house or you can design any building you like, such as a shed, playhouse, garden office, or treehouse!

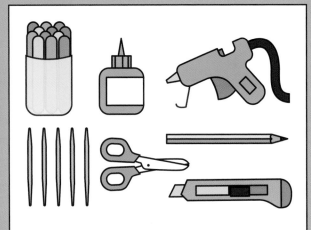

WHAT YOU NEED

- A package of craft sticks
- Superglue or a glue gun
- A pencil
- Scissors or a craft knife
- Toothpicks or wooden skewers

1 Start by making a strong base for your building. Arrange a row of craft sticks side by side to make a square. Glue craft sticks on top at right angles to make a double layer.

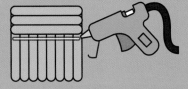

2 To make a wall, arrange a row of craft sticks together to make a rectangle. Glue a craft stick at a diagonal angle to hold them all together.

3 For a wall with windows, make a row of craft sticks the same size as the first wall. Lay another craft stick on top at right angles. Draw a line on it at the edge of the craft sticks.

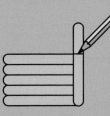

4 With the help of an adult, cut along the line several times with a craft knife. Snap the end off the craft stick. Make two more sticks the same length. Glue the three short sticks across the other sticks: one on each edge and one in the middle. Make sure you don't put glue on two of the long middle sticks.

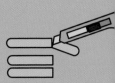

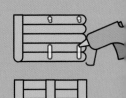

5 Pull out the unglued craft sticks to leave window spaces. Use pieces of toothpick or wooden skewer to make window panes. Repeat steps 3 to 5 to make a third wall.

6 Glue the walls onto the base and to each other at the sides. A typical summer house is open at the front.

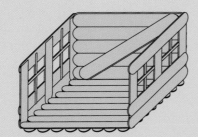

7 Make a roof by making two flat panels that are a similar size and shape to the walls. Make two "A" shapes from craft sticks, slightly wider than the summer house.

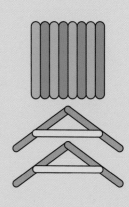

8 Make little notches on the sides of two craft sticks with scissors, as shown. Glue them across the tops of the side walls, leaving the notches above the craft stick underneath. Sit the A-frames into the notches. Glue them in.

9 Glue the roof panels onto the A-frames and to each other in the middle. Place your summer house in your garden.

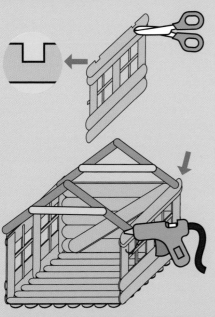

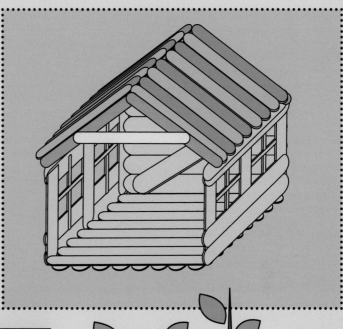

TAKE IT FURTHER

For a treehouse, you need a thick, short, branching stick. Clean it, if necessary, and let it dry. With an adult's help, push it into the ground or stand it in a pot of pebbles to hold it in place.

Build a treehouse the right shape and size to fit between the branches. Glue it in place or use string to tie it on. You can also use more sticks to make stilts to support the treehouse. Finally, add a rope ladder, made from string and pieces of toothpick.

FINISHING TOUCHES

Add the finishing touches to your garden with a fence to go around it, a path, seats, and decorations. You can make all of these or just choose the ones you like.

First make sure everything you've made for your garden is arranged how you want it. If possible, leave spaces between different areas for paths and garden furniture.

FENCE AND GATE

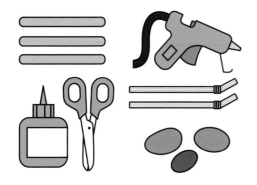

WHAT YOU NEED

- Lots of wooden craft sticks
- Superglue or a glue gun
- Scissors
- Two bendy straws
- Pebbles (optional)

1 To make a fence, arrange several craft sticks in a row. Glue two sticks across them at the top and bottom to hold them together.

2 Leave some space on the two vertical sticks at the edges, so you can add more sections of fence and glue them together.

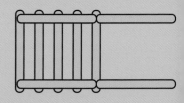

3 Stand sections of fence around the edges of the garden, just inside the tray. Use pebbles to hold the fence in place.

4 For a gate, make a separate section of fence. Cut off the long ends of the bendy straws. Glue the bendy sections to the fence and the gate to make bendy hinges.

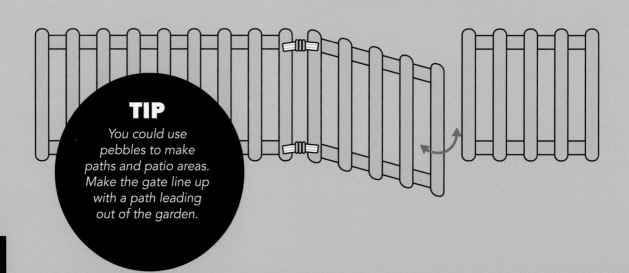

TIP
You could use pebbles to make paths and patio areas. Make the gate line up with a path leading out of the garden.

GARDEN FURNITURE

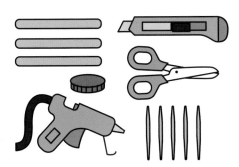

WHAT YOU NEED

- Wooden craft sticks
- Toothpicks
- Scissors or craft knife
- Superglue or a glue gun
- A plastic bottle lid (optional)

1 To make a seat, cut two short sections of craft stick about 1 inch (2.5 cm) long, using scissors or a craft knife.

2 Glue the pieces together in a seat shape. Stick pieces of toothpicks to the bottom to make legs.

3 Try using larger pieces of craft stick to make benches or tables. You could make a round table from a plastic lid, with toothpick legs.

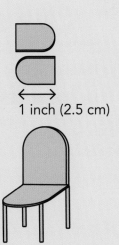

1 inch (2.5 cm)

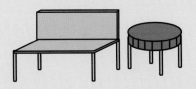

BUNTING

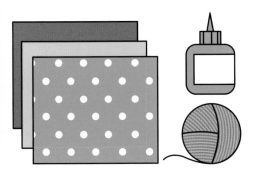

WHAT YOU NEED

- String or strong sewing thread
- Paper, felt, or fabric scraps in different colors
- Glue

1 Cut lots of small diamond shapes, about 1 inch (2.5 cm) long, in different colors. Cut a piece of string the length you want.

2 Fold the diamonds over the string to make triangles. Glue the two sides together.

3 Tie the bunting between different parts of the garden, such as the summer house, greenhouse, or fence.

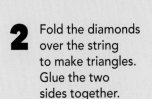

1 inch (2.5 cm)

AND HERE IS YOUR FINISHED GARDEN!

GLOSSARY

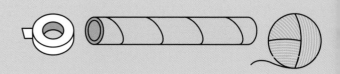

biosphere A building in which a biome (a community of plants and animals) is recreated, such as a rain forest or woodland

botanical gardens A garden where plants are grown to be studied and displayed

carbon dioxide A gas found in the air and used by plants to grow

drip tray A large shallow tray for holding plants in pots

dwarf varieties Small varieties of garden plants

glue gun An electric tool that heats up to melt and apply strong glue

greenhouses Clear glass or plastic buildings that collect heat, for growing plants

hydroponics A method of growing plants without soil, in trays of liquid

oxygen A gas found in the air and given out by plants

pentagon A shape with five straight sides

photosynthesis The process in which plants use sunlight to produce food for themselves using water and carbon dioxide.

plant sticks Thin wooden, plastic, or bamboo sticks used to hold up growing plants. Also called plant stakes

or supports.

seed heads Parts of plants that contain seeds after the plant has flowered

seedling A very young plant that has grown from a seed

seedpod The parts of some types of plants that contain seeds and split open when the seeds are ripe

wildflowers Local flowering plants that grow naturally

FURTHER INFORMATION

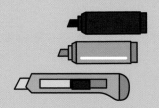

WHERE TO GET MATERIALS

Everyday items
You'll probably have some everyday items and craft materials at home already, such as paper towels, plastic wrap, pens, string, paper and cardboard, clear tape, glue, and scissors.

Recycling
Old packaging that's going to be thrown away or recycled is a great source of materials, such as cardboard boxes, yogurt containers, ice-cream tubs, plastic bottles, and colorful paper packaging.

Grocery stores
Great for basic items you might not have at home, such as straws, toothpicks, and some garden items, such as soil, seeds, and pots.

Outdoors
Collect item such as twigs, sticks, stones, and shells for free!

Specialty stores
Craft stores and garden centers are useful for things like a craft knife, a glue gun, acetate, modeling clay, fabric, beads, buttons, garden trays, pots, seeds, small plants, soil, sand, and pebbles. If you don't have the store you need near you, ask an adult to help you search online.

Thrift stores
It's always a good idea to check thrift stores when you can, because they often have all kinds of handy household items and craft materials at very low prices.

BOOKS

Aloian, Molly. *Green Gardening and Composting*. Crabtree Publishing, 2014.

Appleby, Matthew. *The Children's Garden: Loads of Things to Make and Grow*. Frances Lincoln, 2016.

Archer, Joe, and Caroline Craig. *Plant, Cook, Eat!: A Children's Cookbook* Charlesbridge, 2018.

Biggs, Emma and Steven Biggs. *Gardening with Emma: Grow and Have Fun*. Storey Publishing, 2019.

WEBSITES

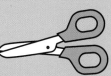

PBS Design Squad
pbskids.org/designsquad
Visit this site for lots of great design and build challenges.

Gardeners' World Projects for Kids
www.gardenersworld.com/how-to/grow-plants/10-gardening-projects-for-kids
10 fun and easy garden projects to try.

Kids Gardening
https://kidsgardening.org/
This website has gardening games, facts, and activities for kids.

INDEX

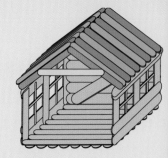